Emotional
Options

ISBN: 0-9760901-3-9
Personal Gowth/Self-Help

MORGAN · JAMES
PUBLISHING FOR THE REST OF US...
www.morganjamespublishing.com

Printed in the United States of America

ABOUT EMOTIONAL OPTIONS

"The hands-down ultimate guide to happiness in a belief driven world. Freeing, magical, empowering, and unforgettable! Way ahead of its time."

JOE VITALE
Author of *The Attractor Factor*

"Original, strong and absolutely on the mark. It is power packed."

JANE CLAYPOOL
Author of *Wise Women Don't Worry,*
Wise Women Don't Sing the Blues

"Not another cheer-up-and-think-positive book, but a cutting edge technique to resolve self-defeating beliefs that can shape a whole life and never be addressed."

JEFFREY PEASE
Magical Blend Magazine

"I've been involved with the psychotherapeutic nature of medicine for the last twenty years and the Option Method is by far the most powerful tool I've come across. This book is a superb introduction."

EDWARD TAUB, M.D.
Author of *Balance Your Body, Balance Your Life*

"It's beautiful. I finished it eager for more, much more! I especially like the simple straightforward presentation. Its honesty, which is so much like you, is, of course a pleasure."

BRUCE DI MARSICO
Founder of the Option Method

"With *Emotional Options*, I've been able to teach the Option Method to individuals and groups in the U.S. and abroad. It is unique and insightful. I'm delighted to see a new expanded addition. If you value happiness, read this book. It can change your life."

LENORA S. BOYLE
Option Method Trainer

ABOUT TRAVELLING FREE

"Mandy Evans' work with belief systems is strong and clear. She helps people to overcome their own self-defeating beliefs in an empowering way."

JOHN GRAY
Author of *Men Are From Mars,*
Women Are From Venus

"*Travelling Free* gives insight into freedom from victimization through out-worn memories—to use your memories without allowing your memories to use you."

DEEPAK CHOPRA, M.D.
Author of *The Seven Spiritual Laws Success*

"*Travelling Free* bridges the gap between the psychological approach to wellness and the recovery model of "twelve-step" programs. The simple, yet creative exercises can be done by anyone, anywhere."

EAST WEST MAGAZINE

"What this reviewer enjoyed most about this book is its readability, user friendliness, and delightful sense of humor...rarely has personal growth been so much fun."

MEDITATION MAGAZINE

"This little book offers a way to explore and dissolve self-defeating beliefs, let go and move toward what you want now."

SMALL PRESS REVIEWS

"Evans has written a unique and helpful guide for a journey whose only destination is a happy here and now."

THE LIGHT CONNECTION

Emotional Options

Mandy Evans

2004

*Dedicated to Marvin Beck,
Mima Cataldo, Gene Gittlesen,
Jan Kiss, and Yosaif August
—what a group!*

Acknowledgements

The people who have worked with me taught me more with their courage and open minds than I find words to tell. Their explorations have woven themselves into the fiber of my teaching and my being.

Anne Grete Mazziotta, Jeffrey Pease, Catherine Rush, Debra Lux, Karling Kolter, Sandra Lewis, Lorraine McGrane, Martin Parks, Sheila Haff Bradley, Maureen Rafael, David Hanson, Elijah Liebowitz, Sonia Gunderson, Harriet Glubka, Clare Rosenberg, Ava Brenner, Georgie Birch, Rae Bales, Cary Loose, Renata De Angelis, Ruth Hirsch, Reggie Moser, and Verone Lawton have been exceptional students and teachers.

Lenora Boyle learned Option from the inside out. She teaches with insight, broad experience, and generosity of spirit—what greater compliment can you pay a teacher?

Bruce Di Marsico, founder of the Option Method, taught me how to be happier and how to help other people to become happier too. I cannot imagine what my life would be like if I had not met him.

Douglas Wilson, director of the Rowe Conference Center in Massachusetts, hired me years (and many Rowe seminars) ago. He stood up for me at a time when it really counted. He sets an example in courage, wisdom, and integrity.

Sheila Haff Bradley, Catherine Rush, Barnaby Dorfman, and Ava Brenner combed these pages improving clarity and sleuthing out typos. Ann Epner read the manuscript and offered helpful suggestions.

Thank you all so very much!

Contents

Emotional Options

Foreword by Joe Vitale

You Never Know

Eighteen years ago I answered a classified ad that changed my life.

It was maybe three lines in the back of a magazine. Nothing special about it. It said if you want Option Method sessions, contact Mandy Evans. I'm still not sure why I replied. Curiosity was in the air. My inner guidance system said do it. I did.

I wrote Mandy and asked if she had any tapes of her talks. Though Mandy didn't tell me at the time, she thought my request a little over the edge. She didn't have anything for sale. The tapes she had were originals. She'd have to dig them out and duplicate them. And for who? Some unknown guy who answered her little ad? But I persisted. Mandy eventually made a few tapes for me.

I didn't like them. I LOVED them. I told her they were the best things I had ever heard. I still remember Mandy's happy voice, light vibe, and clear message. I said she was basically 99% belief-free, like coffee that is 99% caffeine-free. She was a breath of fresh air, a voice from a happy place. I couldn't wait to meet her.

I shared her tapes with a friend of mine. He was equally impressed. Together we sponsored an Option Method workshop and brought Mandy to us.

We ended up having one of the most beautiful weekends of our entire lives, all of us exploring our beliefs with the bubbly Mandy as our guide.

And now look. Mandy and I have been friends for almost two decades. Her books have gone through several editions and continue to change lives. Since I'm the author of numerous books, I like to think I had something to do with inspiring Mandy to write these refreshing works of hers. Whether I did or not, I'm elated that she wrote them. They are wisdom in book form, and contain the key to unlock your own well-being.

And look at today. Eighteen years later I'm writing the foreword to her little masterpiece.

Ah! You never know what life will present to you when you come from happiness, and curiosity, and aren't afraid to answer a small classified ad in the back of an old magazine.

Be happy now.

Joe Vitale
www.MrFire.com

Why the Options Are Emotional

A man from Houston, Texas contacted me to present a seminar for his company. He began with hearty enthusiasm, eager to sign me up. I told him that the seminar for that year was called *How to Exercise Your Emotional Options.* "Oh," he said. He sounded seriously disappointed. "Couldn't it be about some *uther* kinda options?" He said he would get back to me but I never heard from him again.

He was not the first person to react that way either. Lots of people just plain do not want to deal with their emotions. They don't want to feel them. They don't want to talk about them. They say things like: "It's not business-like; it won't get you anywhere or do you any good anyway." Most people I talk to have no clue that they can change their feelings without taking medication, illegal drugs or making big changes in their circumstances.

So why not just do what the guy asked and make it about some other kind of options? Here is why.

What if I told you that you could be happier right now, even before you fix all of the things that seem wrong with your life or our world? What if choosing happiness were a real option you could exercise over and over again? What if emotional freedom could be yours if only you knew how to claim it?

What if maybe, just maybe, the lion's share of anger, guilt, fear and, other painful emotions could change to eagerness, awareness or peace?

Over the last thirty-five years I have witnessed thousands of people make those changes. And yet I know millions more feel miserable as they struggle to make more money, find true love or achieve worldwide recognition. Why? Many of them have lost track of why, but if you ask them it usually turns out they just want to feel better and they believe that achieving those goals is what it will take.

This is the point where I want to wave banners, stand on rooftops and shout, "If you don't like the way you feel, deal with the feeling first!" You can do it! Deal with the feeling of explosive anger even before you express it, much less act on it. Handle guilt or fear before you let it hold you back from life's adventures. Before you make a life-changing move in order to feel better, before you go on a diet, resort to drugs, tell your boss off, quit your job, file for divorce or leave town—deal with the feelings first!

Because whether we like it or not, emotions are the rocket fuel of manifestation. From people who teach visualization techniques to overcome serious diseases to motivational speakers who command enormous corporate fees, the word is out. Whatever it is you want to achieve, you've got to feel it first.

This mysterious law of the universe works whether you are aware of it or not, whether you believe it or not. Whether or not you consciously practice it, your emotional state always has and always will have a profound effect on what happens next in your life.

The choices you make and actions you take when you are afraid lead down a different road from the choices and actions you take when you are happy.

The solutions you find to a problem when you feel guilty will not be the same ones you come up with when you feel at peace.

Those of us for whom happiness is the road less traveled may face a tangle of circumstances and relationships now. I sure did. Becoming happier helps to make better choices from this point on. It also helps to deal with the results of actions taken during more painful times.

That's the cause part of the equation—feelings actually cause things to happen. Feelings influence events.

Here is the result part. Getting, doing, having stuff is nice. Fame, fortune, and good looks stand out among the most popular getting-stuff goals. But there is not a whole lot of correlation between getting stuff and happiness. I worked with a woman who told me she walked down the aisle to receive a GRAMMY award listening to a voice in her head repeat "You don't deserve this. You don't deserve this." Another client managed to maintain an abiding resentment about earning only

$140,000 a year plus options at his job. A famous Hollywood beauty confessed that she dreads losing her looks so much that she knows no peace or happiness. These extreme "fame, fortune and good looks" examples demonstrate that getting stuff will not produce the happiness that Madison Avenue, Hollywood and Wall Street would have us believe it does.

We all know people who stand out in their talent, financial achievement, beauty, or mighty deeds but are not happy.

The mind-boggling part is that they do not want to be happy—yet! They do not know that happiness is a real option for them or how to choose it.

Your emotional experience of life is so important. As we wander about this paradise called earth, the perception of what happens to us combines with our thoughts and beliefs about what it means. That ever-changing combination produces emotional responses. When we feel curious, grateful, loving, or happy, life seems like a precious gift. But if you are ridden with guilt, filled with fear, so angry that no love can enter your heart, or so resentful that joy is only an irritating word, then life is more like hell on earth. What good are fame, fortune, and good looks in hell?

Exercising your emotional options allows you to experience life on your own terms in the most real way possible. It's like magic. You can create the result first. You can be happy even before you change all of those things you want to change.

That is why the options are emotional.

*Are you as happy as
you would like to be?*

Emotional Options

How It Works

Each of us lives by our own private belief system, our own version of reality. Those beliefs determine how we feel in ways I never heard about during the most painful years of my life.

Years of therapy never touched on it. I even got half way through a certificate program in group counseling without a clue that the key to happiness rested in my own beliefs.

Looking back over thirty plus years of working with this belief/emotion connection, it appears no one else is hearing much about it either.

Everyone has a belief system. Some beliefs are conscious; we know we have them. A conscious belief system generates power. An unconscious belief system generates power too, but in a reactive, bouncing-off-the-walls-as-you-go way that leaves a lot of wreckage to deal with. Some of the beliefs that we live by without knowing it play havoc with our emotions, our actions, and every aspect of our lives.

Have you ever alienated someone you love with explosive anger? Or paralyzed yourself with fear of rejection? If so, you know what it is like to feel trapped in an emotional cage. There is a way out.

If you have ever tried to overcome depression by feeling bad about being depressed, you know what it is like to operate with a self-defeating belief, though you probably don't know that you are doing it.

If you have ever felt guilt in an attempt to change a behavior in yourself or in someone else, then you know what it is like to try something that does not work. The harder you try, the worse it gets. You can't even tell if you haven't felt guilty enough yet to make yourself mend your wicked ways so there is no clue when to stop.

A hidden nest of self-defeating beliefs operates in each of these examples. Neither approach works very well and if it does, the toll is much too high. There is a better way.

"Into each life a little rain must fall" may be true, but do we have to suffer each time we get wet? Often we drench ourselves with painful feelings that are totally unnecessary.

We can become happier, more at ease with ourselves and better able to create new options than we may have dared to dream possible. The next chapters lay out a simple, easy to follow, step-by-step way to identify, explore and resolve the self-defeating and conflicting beliefs that keep us stuck in pain.

The importance of our belief systems and the role they play in our lives becomes more apparent every day. People, who once scoffed at the notion that what you believe has something to do with what happens to you, now speak seriously about changing beliefs. But how?

A belief is simply something that seems true to you. It may be a conclusion you arrive at based on the seeming evidence at hand. It could be something you were told and had no reason to doubt. The dictionary says it is "the acceptance of certain things as true and real."

We form beliefs all the time. These beliefs weave together to form our individual belief systems—our own private versions of reality. Many of them are simply not true. Others conflict with each other.

One large group of them dictates our emotional responses.

These are some of the beliefs and systems of belief you can use this book to uncover and dismantle:

- Waiting for Happiness Beliefs:

"How many of you are as happy as you would like to be right now?" I begin talks with that question sometimes. Usually a few hands go up. Then I ask, "What are the rest of you waiting for?"

A few people chuckle and a whole lot of hands go up. When I call on the people holding their hands in the air, they tell us their reasons for waiting to be happy. The list of things people require before they will be happy grows with each talk. A favorite is the woman in Texas who drawled "Ahm waitin'

9

for my husband to be nice." He had sponsored the talk.

These people believe they have good reasons for postponing happiness. But do they? What do any of us gain by waiting to be happy? What harm would we cause if we jumped the gun and rejoiced now?

- Events Control Your Feelings Beliefs:

Examples of these beliefs abound. Media psychologists ask their TV and radio patients, how does that *make* you feel?

You can read it in your local newspaper every day. A quick scan of mine turned up these headlines, which I pasted together and blew up as a visual guide for workshops:

Roar of leaf blowers enrages city

McCallum subsidies anger some residents

Situation angers residents, costs businesses

All of those headlines describe some mysterious out-break of residential anger over which the poor citizens have no control. Right there in bold Helvetica type presented as statements of fact. You won't find many of them about other emotions. "If it's rage, it tops the page" must be the headline equivalent to the old journalism rule, "if it bleeds, it leads."

The very structure of our grammar holds these events-make-you-feel beliefs as in the phrase it angers or it saddens. But how does the anger really happen? The headlines above omit an important part of the equation—what the citizens believe about the leaf blowers' roar. The neighbor who loves the cleaned up sidewalks welcomes it gladly. The one who can't hear well does not mind at all. And *you* can feel any way you please whether you like leaf blowers or not.

- Beliefs About Anger:

Mahatma Gandhi may have felt righteous anger or indignation when Indians were denied access to such a basic staple as salt. We know that the great non-violent leader saw the injustice. He responded with great energy and determination. He changed the world. Yet Gandhi is known as a peaceful man, not for keeping himself in a permanent state of indignation.

Martin Luther King also recognized injustice and worked to overcome it. He spoke out with passion. He too changed our world, but he did not rant and rave with the rage that devours from within and inflicts intentional pain on others.

Neither of these great leaders found a need to preset their anger and hold it in place in order to accomplish near miracles.

But what about regular people like us? If Charlie, (we'll call him) believes people will walk all over him unless he gets angry when he disagrees with them, Charlie will spend a lot of time really ticked off. Unless that belief changes, we can predict Charlie's emotional response to disagreements fairly accurately.

If Charlie also believes that he will never stop being angry unless he gets really mad at himself about it, the poor guy will be angry even more of the time.

If Charlie believes that he will not be careful unless he is afraid, he will experience more fear than you or I will.

If Charlie believes that he needs to feel guilty or else he will never stop a behavior he wants to change, our Charlie will be one guilt-ridden guy.

- Beliefs About Changing Circumstances:

These beliefs tell us that in order to change the way you feel, you have to change your life. Or even more challenging, you have to change someone else's life.

Friends may say, "If you feel bad, do something about it," because they think a change in circumstances offers the only hope of feeling better.

- Life Extinguishing Beliefs:

Bruce Di Marsico originated the Option Method on which this book is based. He used the phrase, "life extinguishing" beliefs in a class I took. It sent chills of recognition down my spine.

Over the years I have heard thousands of them. Now, as people talk, what they believe comes through as loudly as what they say. If you listen for them, the hidden beliefs that determine how people feel and what they do become increasingly obvious and important. Do the beliefs you hold enhance your life or extinguish it?

- Beliefs About Punishment:

In workshops and interviews people often ask if there are widely held social beliefs that cause unhappiness. This next set of beliefs stands out among all of the others like a beacon that flashes, "Change me! For the good of all humankind, change me!!"

How can you punish a cat? One sweet summer morning, before September 11, 2001, when no disasters befell the world, the news was kind of slow. ABC News anchors Diane Sawyer and George Stephanopolis struggled through an uninspired piece about animal training. They were dying up there on the small screen. Maybe that is why Ms. Sawyer blurted out, "I trained my cat to, um, er, go potty in the toilet." A long pause followed, an unusually long pause, a TV eternity of a pause. A baffled look spread over the former presidential press secretary's face. "But, how do you punish a cat?" asked George.

A big assumption (or belief) lurks there. Let's play "Find The Hidden Belief." What does George's remark tell us that he believes about punishment and learning? It says that you need to punish in order to teach and be punished in order to learn.

Think of all the suffering that pair of beliefs causes in the world.

Most animal trainers removed punishment from their teaching methods only recently. They saw it as needlessly cruel and counter-productive. For example, people who train or work with chimpanzees for scientific reasons routinely used electric shock as part of the program until a few years ago. Then they discovered that the little guys responded just as well to repetition, rewards and encouragement. Horse whisperers and dog trainers follow the same principles with excellent results.

Hopefully some day we will agree that these kinder methods work for teaching human beings too, especially children. The phrase "I'm going to teach you a lesson!" would take on a whole new meaning.

Faith in the value of punishment takes many forms that impact our lives in countless destructive and limiting ways. Whether we punish to get even, or punish to change, punish to teach or punish to deter—the toll is high, the results open to dispute.

I want to interject an idea here before we go further into these beliefs. Each of us reacts to punishment, or intended punishment, in different ways. Perhaps the ideas in this book and practicing the Option Dialogues that follow will help you to gain more freedom over how you feel. When someone tries to make you feel bad, to humiliate you, or actually inflicts physical pain, you will know more about your emotional options and how to exercise them.

The goal is to bring awareness to the ways our faith in punishment often surpasses our faith in creativity, love, and perseverance. Here are some of the many ways society's belief in the value of punishment manifests itself:

The Chiding Inner Monologue: This mind chatter mutters things like, "You stupid jerk. Can't you do anything right?" while you forge stoically ahead trying to accomplish whatever the task-at-hand may be. Most inner reprimands include some sizzling X-rated language to give them that extra oomph. Ever catch yourself doing that? I cannot believe I still do it—and often. Now I'm on to myself though. I find it mildly amusing. Sometimes I actually counter out loud, "Don't be ridiculous; I am not a stupid jerk. I am actually very bright." Or grinningly repeat the childhood singsong, "Am not, am not, am not!"

Verbal Abuse Directed at Someone Else: Pity the customer service representatives who listen to people yell at them people all day long. How often do you hear people, who believe they have been wronged, simply state what they would like instead of what they got? When you want someone to fix something, change something, be more like the person *you* had in mind, all too often the reproach approach dominates.

Physical Abuse: From spanking a child to the abuse of prisoners, the belief that intentionally in-

15

flicting pain works is still widely held. Two favorite authors dispute this, Doctor Spock in his classic, still in print and going strong book, *Baby and Child Care* says, "discipline does not mean punishment." Peter Eikann lays out a strong case in, *The Tough on Crime Myth,* which is unfortunately out of print now. Amazon.com lists several used copies for sale though.

Torture and Death: Taken to the extreme, faith in punishment leads to torture and death.

When it comes to life-enhancing beliefs and life-extinguishing ones, surely beliefs about punishment rank at the top of the list of beliefs we can hold that extinguish our aliveness—moment by moment, or altogether in death.

All sorts of false beliefs can produce strong emotional reactions that make life extremely painful. Other beliefs will hold a particular emotion in place long after it has served any useful purpose. Still other beliefs limit us like the bars of a small prison cell.

Beliefs that foster or allow happiness enhance life. Beliefs that foster or cause un-happiness extinguish life. Can it be that simple? With a smile, I believe it is.

What do you do if you suspect you hold beliefs that may undermine your health and happiness? Adapt them? Adopt somebody else's?

Trying to superimpose a new belief system over what already seems true to you does not work. That is because your belief system represents your version of reality—your unique, private reality, handed down through generations and cultures, cultivated since birth and added to by your own conclusions and observations every moment. Your reality does not change because someone tells you it is bad for you.

Should you try to figure out which ones are positive and which ones are negative? How would you even know which ones to try to change if you knew how to do it? You can't exactly get up in the morning and start with "Do I believe I'm awake? Do I believe this is planet earth? Do I believe I can stand up?" You would never get out of bed.

Well then what *can* you do then when you suspect that your own beliefs stand in your way in an important area of your life?

If we abandon the defense of our existing beliefs and search for truth instead we will learn more.

You can learn how to uncover those beliefs— especially the hidden ones you do not even know you have. Then you can explore them, find out if they are true for you, and how to change them if they are not.

The real miracle is that you can feel better now. Feeling better offers a bonus. We make our greatest contributions when we are happy. When we are relaxed our bodies heal themselves and maintain health better. Every time we declare emotional independence from circumstances and events we free creativity and energy to deal with whatever conditions we encounter. We see more clearly. New directions become obvious that once were hidden in a red blaze of anger or the cold gray of despair.

I divided our work into four basic aspects:

Attitude: Acceptance

The Dialogue

Desire: Your Inner Sense of Direction

Self Trust/Self Authorization

These four aspects weave together to allow us to engage with this basic idea: You are the expert in the matter of your own life. If you feel some way you don't like feeling, perhaps it is because you believe that you have to, in order to be true to yourself for example. Or perhaps you believe you need to feel that way in order to get what you want or that it is the only way *to* feel.

Let's look together to first discover how you feel. Then we will find out why you feel that way—what beliefs govern those feelings. We will learn how to question those beliefs to find out if they are true for you or not. Perhaps you can be happier now, even before you fix everything you think is wrong with you and our world.

Emotional freedom is the primary goal; to me that is happiness. Your own definition is the one that counts here. Some people call it:

- Peace

- A sense of oneness with the universe

- Enlightenment

- Joy

- Bliss

- Ecstasy

- Aliveness

- Freedom to be yourself

- Feeling exactly the way I want to feel

Basically, happiness is whatever you got up this morning for. It is what you hope will happen as a result of everything you do, everything you strive for and everything you achieve.

What kinds of feelings does *Emotional Options* work with? Fortunately the happy ones do not require any work. That leaves any unwelcome feeling.

I cannot think of any reason to characterize an emotion as positive or negative. It seems like a politically correct way to say good feelings and bad feelings. How can you begin to tell which emotions are positive and which ones are negative? What benefit would you gain from judging them in that way? Before you could tell whether feelings are positive or negative, wouldn't you have to know where the feelings come from, what they are for, what they will lead to, and the answers to a host of other questions? I don't know the answers to those questions. I do not know anyone else who knows them either.

People get better and more long-lasting results when they skip the positive/negative assessments and accept their feelings for the moment. That way they can explore them and the beliefs that fuel them.

Here are three good ways to choose what to work on. If you don't like feeling the way you feel and you cannot say you would choose the feeling, it is probably a good emotion to explore. You probably did choose the feeling in some way you are not aware of, but we will deal with that later. The second excellent clue is if you suspect an old familiar emotional response gets in your way. A third helpful hint is if you want something but you believe that although other people can have it, you cannot.

Most of us have one or two predominant, painful emotional states we return to over and over. They work like preset default states (to borrow from computer terminology) that take over every time circumstances line up in a certain way. One person, for instance, may feel afraid every time she tries something new, though someone else may always feel excited.

Someone told me that her father was "a bit of a drinker and womanizer." When he was late getting home her mother always gathered her sister and her around the kitchen table and said, "Girls, we've got some serious worrying to do."

One of us always feels a sense of shame associated with rejection if he is not chosen quickly when partnerships or groups form, though another always gets sad. In another common emotional default state, some of us always struggle with anger when we cannot get what we want, even though we may see the toll it takes on our relationships.

Remember, beliefs we hold that we are usually not aware of govern these emotional default states. If the beliefs change the emotional responses change too. When we free ourselves from these automatic emotional responses we become emotionally conscious. We open ourselves to experiences and creativity far beyond what most of us have thought possible.

What painful or life-diminishing feelings do you recognize as emotional default states for you— guilt, fear, shame, sadness, anger, rage, envy, resentment, frustration? Or?

Free-flowing emotions sweep through us at every moment. They contribute to the full range of human experience. Most emotions come and go in a way that makes life more interesting, like a good movie. No problem, nothing to work on.

Like that default state on a computer, preset emotions like the "serious worrying" the mother and her daughters practiced at the kitchen table seem to have a life of their own.

Here are some examples of these two different kinds of emotions.

The awareness of danger is different from fear. Awareness of danger generates a healthy flight-or-fight response. Senses quicken. Adrenalin splashes into the body. Everything needed to wage battle or escape harm falls into place. When the danger passes—victory or escape achieved, a whole bunch of new emotions enliven the theatrical production called life. But countless people, because of beliefs they are not aware of, preset their fear and hold it actively in place as if that keeps them safe. Imagine trying to relax if you believed that you need to be afraid in order to protect yourself from danger. Think of the toll it would take on your body, your relationships, and any other aspect of life you can think of.

The first free-flowing fight or flight response enhances life. The second fixed, holding fear in place and active, extinguishes life. It is like the difference between the heightened alert response described by a rock climber scaling a sheer face and the abiding fear that keeps someone else from ever attempting such an adventure.

An awareness of our own wrongdoing can lead to beneficial changes in behavior, but abiding guilt destroys far more than it helps.

An awareness of loss is a far cry from the feeling of devastation that comes when you add the belief, "I would be a terrible person if I ever felt good again after this." Or "my chances for happiness are gone too." Those beliefs stand guard against enjoying anything at any time.

I have never worked with anyone who suffered from a strong, problematic feeling who could not find an equally problematic belief, or snarled nest of beliefs, that proved false when we explored them.

Do beliefs govern all of our feelings? I doubt it. But I know for certain that what you believe plays a strong and overlooked role in everything you feel.

We confront a vast tapestry of causes, effects, things we know, theories, and mysteries. Addiction presents a unique set of challenges. Depression and grief are two deeply complicated and mysterious emotional states.

Addiction: When people ask if Option works with addiction, I tell them that the Twelve Step Programs, Alcoholics Anonymous (AA) and Narcotics Anonymous (NA) have the best track record and offer the best hope in my experience. Trying to explore your belief system with a chemically altered mind is a tough proposition.

The belief that addicts uncovered most often is that they could never be happy without that drug of choice. Giving up happiness and the hope of happiness is a lot to ask of yourself or someone else. Fortunately clean and sober addicts seem to be as happy as anyone else. I have worked with chemically dependant people who built enough strength and tasted enough hope for happiness to walk into an AA or NA meeting room and ask for help. They got it.

Depression: A young woman in one of my groups suffered terribly from depression. The day I met her, she sat on the floor of a class at a school for holistic health where I taught. She looked up through a tangle of unwashed hair with an expression of such desolation I felt my heart lurch. Clean and sober after years of too much alcohol and an assortment of drugs, she worked hard to rebuild her life as she struggled with exhaustion, despair, and feelings of hopelessness.

After exploring her feelings and beliefs for a few weeks, she reached a point where she could begin to actually choose some of her emotions. One night in an ongoing group, she wept helplessly while working on a problem. I asked, "If you could feel anyway you want to right now, how would you feel?" First, her face brightened. It literally changed before our eyes, becoming luminous. I would bet big money that the difference would register on a light meter like the ones photographers use. Then a mischievous smile appeared. "I've always been very fond of ecstasy," she said, fully engaged and glowing with it. We watched this transformation wide-eyed.

The feelings we call depression came back though. They were not so overwhelming any longer and moments of happiness broke through more and more often. She knew hours of peace for the first time in years. Still, that heavy feeling of despair returned to drag her down as if it had a life of its own. Now she puzzled with amazement, "If I can *choose* ecstasy and I *know* I can choose it, why on earth would I come up with feeling awful over and over and over?"

One day she got happy enough to want more out of life. Active desire kicked in. The power of happiness coupled with that new desire moved her to consult her doctor. He prescribed Prozac. It worked. It helped her body to re-calibrate. It combined well with her ever increasing time clean and sober and the work she continued to do on her emotional belief-system.

Several years later she called to say, "I'm happier than I ever even imagined I could be. I never dreamed my life could be so good. I thought you'd like to know."

We know a great deal more about the condition called Clinical Depression now than we did just a few years ago. In his fascinating book, *Listening to Prozac*, Peter Kramer traces the rise and fall of serotonin levels in our bodies and the far-reaching effects of that hormone on our emotional well-being. Does that make depression a chemical problem calling for purely medical solutions? Hardly.

In his breakthrough book, *Quantum Healing*, Deepak Chopra reminds us that, "to think is to practice brain chemistry." Every thought that wanders through wherever we think it (that has become an increasingly complicated and controversial issue) causes all sorts of changes. Hormones and neurotransmitters whiz about. They connect with assorted neuroreceptors to create a vast array of results. Then there are all of those beliefs to filter the perceptions through, plus physical and emotional responses to each step in that process. Like water flowing though a valley, this stream of thoughts, beliefs, and feelings alters the landscape of our being.

The influence of energy itself, as used in Acupuncture, Polarity Therapy, Feng Shui, and other disciplines, represents another subject that could fill a library with books.

Rather than engage in debates about the order of chickens and eggs, let's simply intervene on behalf of happiness in the best ways available. One of the most effective ways to do that is one of the least known. When it comes to suffering, a little *belief relief* goes a long way.

Depression is a complicated condition— sometimes over-medicated, sometimes under-medicated, too often ignored. The individual belief systems, that cause us to plunge into emotional and physical distress so often, play a crucial role that has been overlooked almost completely.

The experts who deal with depression, including medical doctors, psychologists, psychiatrists, and social workers learn nothing about belief systems in their training, beyond the placebo effect. That ignorance exacts a heavy toll.

Listening to Prozac by Peter D. Kramer and *Beyond Prozac* by Michael Norton provide a wealth of helpful information on the subject of depression. But you will not find anything about how to reveal the beliefs that play havoc with your emotions in them.

Grief: My mother died slowly from emphysema. She lived longer on less air than she or anyone else thought possible. I thought I would feel relief when she finally left her poor body behind. But when she did, the grief I felt shocked me.

Soon after her memorial service, I set out on a summer tour with my book, *Travelling Free: How to Recover from the Past* and "Exercise Your Emotional Options" talks and seminars. My seminars are strongly experiential, rather than lectures that adhere strictly to prepared material. I only know how to teach by the "we're all in this together" method. I participate and contribute what may be helpful from my own life. The challenge of that summer was to be fully present and give people their money's worth without trying to hide my grief—how to be true to my work and to myself.

During one of the first talks, in a church in Albuquerque, a man asked, "What do you do when *you* feel sorrow or grief?" Tears welled in my eyes. My voice cracked a little as I answered, "My mother died a few weeks ago so I'm feeling it now. I cry often these days. So first I accept myself just the way I am. Then I ask myself what am I crying about? And why? It's mysterious to me. But I know this is how I want to feel."

After the talk church members approached me with hugs, gracious words of support and even thanks for telling the truth. Attendance at the afternoon workshop was higher than expected.

I think we always feel the way we want to feel. But that choice takes place in a context of beliefs we may not be aware of. Very often we disapprove of our feelings so strongly that we try to hide them, change them, or suppress them without ever accepting them and learning what they can teach us.

The main thing I learned that summer was that though it was uncomfortable and certainly inconvenient to grieve while giving a talk on how to be happy, I *consciously wanted* to feel just the way I felt then. And just the way I feel now, which is very different.

Long before that intensely rich and wonderful summer, I had trained with the founder of The Option Method, Bruce Di Marsico, in his original Option Training Group. Then, in the early 1970's, we explored all sorts of universal questions together, like whether or not people *had* to feel certain emotions, especially grief. I had pretty much decided that we did not, but I was not sure.

Then my friend, Steve Antler, told a story that added weight to the don't-have-to-feel-grief side. Steve was hiking in the mountains of Nepal in the early seventies when he stopped to visit a monastery. He met a nun, a western woman who lived there with her young daughter who was about five years old. Fascinated, Steve wanted to know more. He too was on a spiritual journey. But he had promised to meet up with his hiking companion further along the way, so he said his goodbyes and walked on. Weeks later Steve returned that way on his own. He really wanted to spend some time with this woman and learn more about the path that led her to this place. His heart leapt when the monastery came into view in a deep valley below. He saw a short cut leading down to it. He scrambled down the path. It ended in a bramble patch. He retraced his steps to the main path and walked on. He saw several more short cuts and even though he warned himself that they may not work, he could not resist the possibility of arriving before nightfall. He found a dead-end at every shortcut. When darkness fell, he went to sleep by the side of the path.

Steve finally arrived the next afternoon. The members of the community had gathered around the young woman's body chanting and reciting prayers for the dead. The little girl stood beside her mother's lifeless body. Later, radiant with joy, she told Steve, "She was almost a Buddha! She was almost a Buddha! I know she will be next time; I just know it!"

This child lived in a peaceful, spiritual community. She was loved. She never doubted if she belonged, if she was safe. Most of all, she believed her mother had achieved something wondrous, something to celebrate—moving closer to enlightenment and an end to suffering. The child was just happy for her mom.

Steve wrote a poem about the woman he never got to know which ended, "I knew you had lessons to teach me. I had no idea they would be so profound."

Well, that certainly introduced new possibilities! Maybe grief was not necessary or natural after all. Maybe it all depended on what you believed about death, about the prospects for your own life without the person who died and things like that.

That was before the vole encounter. Voles are brown, furry, rat-like creatures that live outdoors—usually. Around 1975, as the weather turned cold, a vole moved into our house. It scurried along the counters in the kitchen. Then it squeezed itself into the cabinet under the sink somehow.

I talked to that vole. I told that vole that he needed to find another place to stay. It paid no attention whatsoever. I threatened it. I told that vole I would set a trap. It continued to meet me in the kitchen. Finally I got a trap. I did not set it, but I put it out and I told that vole its days were numbered if it didn't leave. The vole ignored the warning.

And then I set that trap under the sink.

The next evening my son, Barnaby, and I set out to go to a movie. I forgot my purse. Barnaby ran back into the house to get it while I waited in the car. He was eight years old. When he came out Barnaby was obviously shaken. "Well," he said, "we caught the vole. And there were two of them, Mom. It must have had a mate, because another one came running to the one in the trap and it screamed and screamed. Then it ran out."

See, it wasn't the poor vole in the trap screaming and screaming. That one was dead. The *mate* was screaming and screaming.

I learned two things. Do not set traps for voles. And maybe there is an instinctive, creature anguish we call grief. It's complicated though. Voles mate for life. What was the bereaved vole screaming about? Maybe it dreaded a solitary life that would not be filled with love and companionship, like the life of the little girl in the Buddhist monastery. Do voles have beliefs? What do I know about the life of a solitary vole? Or what causes it to scream when its mate is killed?

Anyone might want to mourn the loss of a child or the death of a mate. But they may not want that loss to diminish their chances for future happiness for all time. Our beliefs about death and loss are open to exploration so that we can feel the way we want to feel, instead of having our emotions determined by an inner set of rules we do not know we live by.

I include these examples to underscore that this book does not aim to tell you what you should feel and what you should not feel—what is normal (that small point on a bell curve) or even what is desirable to feel. The aim here is to expand your emotional options as far as you possibly can. How emotionally free can *you* become?

.

Acceptance is the foundation of Emotional Options. If you aren't accepting, it just won't work, that's all.

The Power of Acceptance

You have to start where you are. Even if that is in despair, fear or anger.

People who are in despair often do not want to feel "happy." They don't have the energy to feel good. It's just too far from where they are to have much appeal. They are already doing the best they can with what they've got and despair is what they have come up with so far. They may, however, want to feel less pain. They may want peaceful rest. From there, they may choose happiness. They can take that journey in a matter of seconds in an atmosphere of acceptance.

By the same token, a frightened person is already doing the best he can. Happiness holds little or no appeal for him. He may, however, welcome a safe haven. He may want to be alert and aware of danger, without fear, if he knows that option exists.

Angry people do not usually really want to be at peace. But if those same people discover that they can be powerful advocates for themselves or their cause without anger, other feelings become more attractive.

The same goes for guilt, shame, anxiety, resentment, and all of the feelings that can be so painful and limiting.

That is why we will cover acceptance first. Feeling less bad may be the first step. If you could feel a little better, then better and better and still remain true to yourself would you like that? If you could become happier and happier and still want what you want, would you welcome that change?

A student of mine, Alice Bruce, defined the process this way. "First you accept them just the way they are, oh, and yourself, of course, and then you ask them gentle, respectful questions about why they are unhappy and then they get stupid and then they smile and feel better." That is pretty much the way it goes.

The ability to exercise your emotional options rests on a foundation of acceptance. Acceptance is the absolute prerequisite to beginning.

Acceptance works better than "being non-judgmental" for several reasons. Which would you prefer, to have someone accept you—or to restrain himself from judging you? Acceptance is active and powerful. It embraces and includes rather than being an exercise in what *not* to do.

To achieve non-judgment *requires* judging. You have to focus on your judgments, become sort of a judgment judge, in order to tell when you are doing it. That distracts from the task at hand.

Acceptance uses a different focus, a different energy. To accept means, "to receive with consent." It can expand to include everything. I can accept you. I can even accept me, with my judgments of you, as long as I know that in this endeavor, my judgments are worthless and best kept to myself. They are just opinions that float through my mind. They have nothing to do with exploring beliefs and feelings. They have no place, no use.

I do not have to judge my judgments or struggle to free myself of them in order to begin. I simply accept them and discard them as unproductive. As the demand dwindles, my supply of judgments decreases as well.

When I began to work with Option in New York City in 1972 a phenomenon occurred that challenged, then stretched my ability to accept things as they are. Sometimes during a session, the room began to get dark then light—dark when their bodies bunched up inside with fear and light when they relaxed inside. Wait! How did I know what happened inside their bodies? I just did. Perhaps anyone would know, if he accepted someone fully and remained focused on that person intently for a length of time. Acceptance is a powerful under-utilized tool.

Sometimes my Option partners said things like "Oh, God, I can't do this," and I would think, "If I can do it, why can't you? It's not even my stuff." But I would ask instead, "Why not?' or "What do you mean?"

Over the next few years I began to see strange and wondrous faces instead of the ones I recognized as the people I worked with. They fascinated me—an Eskimo-looking man, a little boy who could have been from South America—old, old faces, young ones. A woman took on the visage of a male Renaissance poet, or was he a knight? Sometimes people would say, "Don't do that." "Do what?" I would ask, confused and wondering what part of what was happening they referred to. "It's like you can see right through me," one woman said.

A phrase, like an acceptance mantra, came to me. Over and over inside it said quietly, "and that too, and that too," whether lights flashed, faces transformed before my eyes, if my guts wrenched in pain—it just didn't seem to matter. I don't remember ever being afraid, just curious and fully engaged.

I spoke to my friend and fellow Option student, Marvin Beck, about what was happening to me. "Oh, yeah," he said, "I used to feel that stuff too. Then I decided that I didn't have to feel it to know it." That information has served well.

In those early fearless days of exploring human experience I found that a wealth of knowledge becomes available when you accept things the way they are. Let it be. Something happens when you let a thing be the way it is for long enough to look at it that does not happen when your active goal is to make changes. There is a great, and for me, luxurious freedom in being with someone, really seeing him, feeling his presence, hearing him, and seeking only to understand what it is like to be him. That's the foundation of Option. It makes all of the other parts possible. The acceptance we will use in the Option Dialogues manifests as a willingness to perceive reality. Neither approval nor disapproval plays a role. You could call it a neutral awareness with respect.

Remember, to accept means "to receive with consent." It bears no resemblance to resignation.

Imagine someone throwing a ball to you. You can duck it, let it hit you, or catch it and do whatever you like with it. Acceptance is like catching the ball instead of denying it or letting it hit you in the face. You can accept yourself and still want anything you want. You can accept yourself and reach for any goal with all of your strength and desire. You can do the same for anyone you work with. You can accept your Option partner and want for him anything you may want for anyone. You do not need for him to improve in order to feel okay about yourself and your work or about him. This gives both of you enormous freedom to explore, learn, and create.

Unlike resignation or settling for less, acceptance is the starting point from which change can happen.

The biggest challenge in teaching Emotional Options mirrors the biggest challenge in learning Emotional Options: acceptance. How do I help someone to accept herself while she learns what a judgment machine she is? How can a new student grant himself enough acceptance of his fear of not learning to be able to explore that very fear so that he can learn?

How can I communicate more clearly that there is nothing to do in this method but accept yourself and the other person and ask simple, respectful questions to see if it could be okay to be happier now? How can I accept that I have much to learn about all of this and still offer what I do know?

Using Option and teaching it adds richness and happiness to all aspects of my life. The power of acceptance allows me to do that without knowing the answers to all of those questions yet.

Practice Page

1. What is hard for you to accept? Write down whatever comes to mind.

2. Pick one thing that is hard for you to accept to focus on. Write it down.

3. Write the answers to these questions:

   A. What is hard for you to accept about that?

   B. Why is that hard to accept?

   C. What might happen if you felt okay about that?

   D. What do you want instead of what you are upset about?

   E. Do you tend to focus on what you want or on feeling bad about not having it?

What are you un-happy about?

The Dialogue

You may feel some way you don't like feeling. Or you may want something that seems possible for other people but not for you. Those are two really good clues that you hold a self-defeating, limiting, or life-extinguishing belief.

I became aware of those terms in a class at GROW on the Upper West Side of Manhattan in 1971. GROW stood for Group Relations Ongoing Workshops. It offered training in an audacious new approach to work in human relations. As its title says GROW was about groups in the heyday of the 70's group explosion. Sensitivity Training! Encounter Groups! Peer Groups! Women's Groups! Psychodrama, Rational Emotion Therapy, Gestalt Therapy, Poetry, Art, Primal, Rational Emotive, Family and Movement Therapy! If you could do it legally in a group, we did it at GROW.

Who were we? Therapists and counselors eager to learn the latest innovations in psychotherapy. Ministers and priests, nurses, welfare recipients with education grants, parole officers. Fifty youthful offenders from the infamous prison on Riekers Island came in on a bus each morning to join the other assorted seekers of truth and personal growth from all over—and me!

I had returned to school after the breakup of a short, painful marriage, looking to begin a new life and to find a way to support my little boy, Barnaby, and myself.

That day I sat in a circle of chairs next to Sharif, a handsome kid from Reikers Island. His long legs stretched out before him in the jeans those guys got up at the crack of dawn to iron every morning before they boarded the bus for Manhattan. Sharif struggled with whether to identify with this new Black Muslim name or go back to Mike as his mother called him.

This required course, *Overview of Methodologies,* was intended to broaden our awareness about different schools of thought in human relations. I did not like it as much as the other classes I had taken to reach the halfway point in the GROW certificate program in Group Counseling. These overviews offered only a few sessions on each of three different approaches. If we liked it, this little taste left us wanting more. If we didn't like it, those intense interactive group sessions stretched out forever. This week, we began *An Introduction to Option Therapy.* "What's this guy do?" I asked, Sharif. I still remember vividly how I felt—*almost* at home, belonging somewhere for the first time in a long time, glad to be there and grateful to be sitting with a friend.

"No, I heard this one is cool," Sharif answered with a grin.

A man walked in, sat down, and said, "Hi. I'm Bruce. Does anyone have anything they'd like to work on?"

Elsie raised her hand. A groan rumbled around the room. We were in a 70's group at the height of the encounter movement remember, not a tea party. Elsie had worked on many issues in many groups. Most of us had taken at least one course with her. None of us had ever seen Elsie get anywhere on anything, ever. She just seemed to like being the focus of attention until the leader gave up or got mad. It could take a long time.

"What would you like to work on Elsie?" Bruce asked. "My son won't take a bath," she replied promptly.

If people had groaned when she raised her hand, you should have heard the noises that followed that. One young male voice rose above the others in the class. "How old is your son, Elsie?" "Fifteen," she answered. "Don't you think that's a little old to be telling him when to take a bath?" came the snide, melodically intoned retort. In one small question his voice went up and it went down. It slowed and it emphasized in a concert of contempt.

As we chuckled, some in embarrassment and others in agreement, Bruce informed us, "That's not Elsie's problem. Elsie's problem is that her son won't take a bath. If you have a problem with that, we can work on it later."

Wow! Almost all of our teachers talked about respect for the client, but I had never seen a group leader act as if it were true. A curious quiet settled in the room.

Bruce asked Elsie what bothered her about her son's not taking a bath. She told him that she thought it was hard enough to be fifteen without smelling bad.

He continued to ask these questions that I had never heard anyone ask before. In response, Elsie described a painful family scenario of escalating anger and increasing distance between herself and her only child.

Then Bruce asked her what she might be afraid would happen if she weren't angry with her son. "It would mean I didn't love him," she said. "Do you believe that?" he asked. "Yes, she replied, but she sounded confused. There was a quality in her voice I have heard many time since. It signals the breakup of an old painful version of reality before a new happier one forms.

"Do you love your son?" Bruce asked, so gently and respectfully. His tone was just neutral, not leading in any way. Elsie's eyes filled with tears and her mouth began to tremble. Her habitually tense, stiff face softened. "Yes" she said "and I'm afraid I'm losing him." As this odd question and answer dialogue continued, Elsie realized that she did not have to measure her love by the level of her anger. She saw that without anger, she could still try to get that kid to take a bath. She could summon everything she had in her parental arsenal—from withholding TV to bribery.

I had never seen anything like it. Elsie looked like a new person and our rowdy group sat in silent amazement. We had just witnessed our first Option Dialogue. Only it did not have a name yet. "This guy knows something I want to know." I thought.

I signed up for all the Option courses with Bruce Di Marsico I could schedule. There were no books, but we never used books at GROW anyway. Mostly we watched him work with people on their unhappiness, in all of its painful forms. We asked lots of questions. Tempers flared and people debated the causes of unhappiness hotly and sweetly. I was in heaven.

Just as a secret passed around a circle of people alters as it goes around, until it bears little resemblance to the original, I am sure Option has too. Whose is it now? It's ours.

Soon, if you choose, you will have your own version. Bruce offered Option as a gift to us all. When a student in our long ago group asked, "How do you know when you can do it?" he replied with a phrase of the times, "Can you avoid laying a trip on somebody? And ask them some questions about why they're unhappy?" The student nodded that he could. "Then you can do Option," Bruce decreed with a smile.

I began to practice asking these Option questions right away, with anyone who would let me. I began to earn some money, help some people, become much happier myself, and see a future where before there was mostly fear. I got the concepts right away. Living by them was another matter. Isn't that the way it goes?

Decades later, this is how I use those wonderful questions in dialogues with myself and others. The goal is emotional freedom. The steps that follow show how to identify unhappy feelings; how to find the (often hidden) beliefs that fuel them; how to explore those beliefs and see if they are really true. When you see that a belief you have held (maybe for years) is simply not true, doors open and new life-altering possibilities appear.

For our purposes, the term un-happiness (spelled with a hyphen to distinguish it from sadness) is a general word for any form of unwelcome feelings and emotions. It stands for the lack of happiness or emotional well-being.

The steps that follow will make much more sense after you do a few dialogues with yourself or a partner. The most valuable lessons from reading this book will come from your own discoveries about yourself, as you explore your feelings and the beliefs that hold them in place.

How to Do an Option Dialogue

Step One: Acceptance
Accept yourself and the person you work with just as you are. We can call the person who is working on an issue or a problem "the explorer."

Step Two: Identify the feeling or problem
Ask respectful questions to find out if the explorer is feeling some way he does not like feeling. It may be fear, guilt, anxiety, nervousness, or rage, for example. Or it may be a situation or some other problem that he focuses on to begin with. We want to find out what you or the person you work with considers is the issue at hand.

Sample questions to identify the feelings or problem:

- What would you like to work on?

- How are you feeling?

- If you have identified a problem, how do you feel about that?

Step Three: Ask what?
Find out what the person is un-happy about.

Sample questions about what:

- What are you un-happy about?

- What about that involves un-happiness?

Identify and clarify until you both understand what the un-happiness is about. Use their words. For example if your dialogue partner says, "It really ticks me off," Ask, "What about that really ticks you off?" If your partner says, "He makes me crazy," you might ask, "What about that makes you crazy?" Or "What's crazy making about that?" Even though it turns out that the person or event in question is not the cause of the "feeling crazy" simply follow along to get clear about what the explorer thinks is the cause of his un-happiness. If your partner says, "It is just so sad," you could ask, "What about it involves sadness?" The form of un-happiness may be anger, fear, guilt, or another unwelcome feeling. You (or the person you work with) know what is important. You (or that person) are in charge of what is an issue for you.

Sample clarifying questions:

- What do you mean?

- Could you give an example?

- Could you tell more about that?

- What does that mean to you?

Step Four: Ask why?
Find out what the reasons are for feeling that way. These answers tell both of you about the explorer's beliefs. Reasons for being angry or sad, or

fearful are beliefs. These are the beliefs we want to identify so that we can explore them.

At this point we arrive at the only technical term in my version of Option, "getting stupid." That can be a problem. Some people believe that calling their state of mind "stupid" is an excellent reason to get upset. It is, nevertheless, the most accurate term I have found so far. The experience is one of basic, "duhh..." Confronting your own belief system head-on produces this foggy effect of "I don't know nuthin' 'bout no beliefs" Or anything else at the moment!

I have seen whole rooms go into dense fog during the identifying and questioning of beliefs. Many people find it uncomfortable. No one ever taught us to welcome confusion in school. We learned to avoid it with dread and hide it if we could.

Resist the temptation to push through to a premature false resolution just to escape the discomfort of not knowing what will happen—or even what *is* happening at these moments.

I do not know if it is better to wade into the fog, or to wait it out, or back off. So far this has produced the best results: I remain conscious (which can be a struggle). I remember the question (this can be a struggle too) for when they come to and want to hear it again. They couldn't really hear it all the way through the first time. Or I just follow them if they start up again in some way that seems mysterious. Just because I can't see the thread, does not mean it isn't there.

People have interpreted the "getting stupid" in different ways. It probably occurs when one form of reality breaks up and a new one has yet to form. My students quickly learn to welcome the state as a sign of good things to come.

If you ask someone, "Why are you angry about that?' or, "Why do you feel sad about that?" he will often tell you more about *what* he is unhappy about. That is because he may think that what he is un-happy about is *why* he is unhappy. That sentence holds the record for sending the most people into the fog in all of my classes. If you need to read it again (and again!) you are not alone.

Once more we encounter the belief that our unhappiness is the result of events and circumstances, rather than our beliefs and conclusions about those events and circumstances. In other words, the widely accepted belief is that the subject of our un-happiness causes it. I call this "the what to why dilemma." Sometimes it takes patience and persistence to help people to understand the difference between *what* they are unhappy about and *why* they are unhappy about it.

For example, you may be frightened about the loss of a job. Another person may feel angry about that. You might feel sad to learn that a friend has lied to you, but someone else may react with worry. The loss of a job, or the lie told by a friend, are examples of *what* you are un-happy about. Questioning *why* you are unhappy gets into the beliefs and reasons about why anger, or sadness or worry is the way for you to feel. Why is this particular emotion the one for you in this moment?

Sample questions about why:

- Why are you un-happy about that? Or angry, sad, whatever. Use their words.

- Why is un-happy the way to feel about that?

- What does it mean to you?

- What might happen if you weren't un-happy?

- Continue to identify and clarify the feelings, reasons, and beliefs that come up as you go. For example:

  o What do you mean?

  o If (fill in what you are un-happy about) why is that the way to feel?

Step Five: Questioning Beliefs

The answers to the "why" questions will be beliefs. They are the reasons for feeling the unwelcome feelings. Perhaps these reasons, these beliefs will not seem like such good reasons for feeling awful when you explore them.

Beliefs about our lack of worth or right to exist, our chances of being loved, the need to change other people, and about our prospects for ever being happy cause us incalculable emotional pain. In the Option Dialogue, we ask these questions to find out how come we believe things that hurt us or limit us—especially if we don't even know whether those things are true or not.

Don't worry if you agree with your Option partner's reasons for feeling the way he does; it doesn't matter. The explorer's reasons and beliefs count now, not yours. He may break free in an area where you are still stuck. Take a free ride!

Sample questions about beliefs

- Do you believe that?

- Why do you believe that?

- What might happen if you didn't believe that?

- What might become of you if you didn't believe that?

- Do you know if it is true or not?

- Why would you believe something that makes you un-happy if you do not know whether it is true or not?

- What might you be concerned would happen if you did not believe that?

The questions and answers weave around. Follow the lead of the person who is exploring whether that is you or someone else. Even though we enter uncharted territory fraught with getting stupid and fog rolling in, each one of us has the best shot at knowing where we are going.

The answers to, "Do you believe that?" may be things like:

- Yes.

- No.

- Maybe.

- I don't know.

- I'm afraid not to believe that.

- Part of me does.

- Wouldn't anybody?

- Isn't that obvious?

Ask the questions at this point, to discover what you believe and why. Anyone else might have the same feeling or belief too. Let's see why you believe this thing that limits you or causes emotional conflict and un-happiness.

Although it is true that we usually get happier when our beliefs in un-happiness turn into myths before our questioning eyes, getting to "No, I don't believe that" is not the goal. The goal remains to accept, explore, and discover. If you, or an Option partner, see that you want to change a belief that has been held as essential, you will not really explore it. To protect their reality people offer up substitute beliefs. They do this to protect the ones that represent their perceptions of how it really is. If your partner feels pressured into "getting happy" he may pretend to capitulate. It's not the end of the world, but it is an opportunity missed.

It may still seem tempting to just adopt a "better belief" and get it over with. Only you will know that you did that and you will not live by it. Your private inner reality remains the same, only now you added another piece to the puzzle. You don't have to do that, just look and ask; your perceptions will change and so will you.

If you veer off or ask the wrong question (if that is possible) don't worry. It will come around again. It's as if un-happiness were a solid wall. When we begin, it seems the only way to feel. The Option questions peck at that wall looking for a chink, for a way to let a ray of light in. Remember though, to peck with respect for your partner's expertise in the matter of his or her own life.

If you come back to the same place or question a few times without an answer, ask, "Why didn't you answer that question?"

When the answer to "Do you believe that?" changes from "Yes" to "I don't know," a whole new realm of possibility moves into the picture. For example, believing "No one could ever love me," leads to a far different set of life experiences and choices from declaring, "I want to love and be loved even if I do not know yet if anyone loves me or ever could. I would like to find out. I would like to know if I can love and be loved."

Tori Yarbrough, an Option teacher in Colorado Springs called this kind of questioning "sustained, innocent curiosity."

Option really gets exciting when it delves into the nature of individual beliefs. They begin to change, crumble away, or turn into knowing. Reality as we know it breaks up and reforms in a dizzy-making instant. New possibilities appear where before we saw only that solid wall of un-happiness or limitation.

If you want happiness, be happy!

Some Favorite Option Questions

Judi Boggess wrote down the questions she heard me use most frequently in a weekly group I taught in Rosendale, New York. She made a list to share. I added a few and clarified some.

- Are you feeling some way you don't like feeling?

- What are you un-happy about? Identify and clarify.

- What do you mean?

- Why are you un-happy about that? Look for myths and contradictions.

- Do you believe that?

- Does that seem true to you?

- Why do you believe that?

- Do you want to believe that?

- How do you know to believe that?

- Do you believe you would be bad for your-self if you were happy now?

- Do you believe that you would be bad for yourself if you did not feel _____?

- How do you know to feel that? Or to be that?

- How do you know when to get angry, embarrassed, etc.?

- Is it OK for you to be _____?

- If that were so, would you want to know that?

- What are you wanting?

- If you were happy, could you still want that?

- When was the last time you got something you wanted?

- If I could wave a magic wand and your anger (or other feeling) would disappear, would you want me to wave it?

- If there is a better way, why are you unhappy that you have not done that?

- Would you want it to be OK that _____?

- If you were using _____ (a particular feeling) in order to help yourself, how could it help you?

- If you were using _____ (a particular feeling) in order to let yourself know something, what would it be?

- Are you doing the best you can with what you know and what you believe now?

- Did you do the best you could with what you had, or knew or believed then?

As you can see, many of the questions above obviously follow from something said before. With practice you will develop your own style and your own questions to find out why people are unhappy and if they can be happier.

The beliefs we are talking about can shape an entire life and never be addressed.

The One Page Method

Accept yourself and your Option partner just as you are.

Explore by asking respectful questions to find out if it is possible to be happier now. Is un-happiness necessary?

Find out:

1. <u>What are you un-happy about?</u> How do you feel that you don't like feeling? Identify, clarify.

2. <u>Why are you un-happy about that?</u> Identify. What do you mean? Clarify. What might you be concerned would happen if you were not un-happy?

3. <u>Do you believe that?</u> Why do you believe that? What might you be concerned would happen if you did not believe that?

4. <u>Why do you believe that?</u> What might you be concerned would happen if you did not believe that?

Practice Page

1. Identify a feeling you do not like having.

   Are you angry about something? Or irritated? Sad? Frustrated? Nervous? Afraid? Worried? Bothered?

2. Choose one unwelcome feeling and use the One Page Method to explore it.

   Write freely. It can be messy, scattered, or make no sense at all. Follow yourself. Keep writing to help yourself to focus and get through the "getting stupid" phase. A masterpiece can always come later.

   Remember to accept yourself as you are. Allow your emotions to come and go. If your feeling changes to another un-happy one, explore the new feeling.

Desire:
Your Inner Sense of Direction

We can use desire, or our awareness of what we want, as a compass—an inner sense of direction.

When we are in a state of wanting, desiring and aware of what we welcome into our lives, we move toward that experience or attract it to us. We set up a kind of creative tension in the universe, a rubber band effect, between ourselves and the object of our desire. We can also turn emotional tension into creative tension for many reasons.

The confusion between wanting and needing is prevalent. In an Option Training Group at Unison Learning Center in New Paltz, New York, I asked, "You do know the difference between wanting something and being upset about not having it, don't you?" I tossed the question out off-handedly because we had already covered that material.

The whole room "got stupid" together. Only one person, someone who had studied Option for a long time, managed to mummer, "Huh?" The others were gone, far-gone as if in a group trance.

I repeated the question slowly. "You do know the difference between wanting something and being upset about not having it, don't you?"

"Could you ask it one more time?" came the response from the one trainee who could still speak.

Her voice sounded downright sedated. After a third or forth attempt, she said like a flustered child, "Don't say those two same things next to each other anymore. It makes it too weird in my head." We laughed.

The other people woke up, came to, whatever the heck it was, and we went on with the class. They never noticed the exchange or that they had missed something.

At the risk of inducing a trance state I will try it again. There is a difference between wanting something and being upset about not having it.

We can divide the ways to motivate yourself and others into two basic categories:

- Desire and Happiness

- Need and Un-happiness

Motivation with desire and happiness moves things about so quickly that you may not notice it happening.

When we use desire for our motivation, the difference between wanting and attachment becomes clear. Wanting is moving toward and can include happiness. Attachment is often static and requires the feelings of need and sometimes fear, for our very survival. Attachment *appears* to connect us to the object of our need—as if our fear, our sorrow, our guilt, our experience of need, will bring it to us or keep it escaping. But this does not work very well.

To believe that you need something requires, by definition, that you also believe that you cannot be okay without that something. It may be an experience that you believe you need to have or a material object or goal to achieve.

In this need filled view of reality, if you do not get what you want or reach your goal, that very not getting threatens your well-being, your hopes for happiness, and your ability to be okay. When you use "Need and Un-happiness" in order to help yourself to get what you want, you live in that need and un-happiness. That experience is life extinguishing. The very thing you do to help yourself cripples you. It chokes your life force and creativity.

In contrast, the experience of "Happiness and Desire" is life enhancing. It allows happiness now. It fosters a sense of being okay and feeling good. It simply acknowledges that something more or something different would be welcome.

Years ago, I visited a garden with a statue of a particularly jolly Buddha. Inscribed beneath it were the words, "Misunderstood desire is the cause of all suffering." *Misunderstood* desire. At last it made sense!

We have all heard the familiar quote, "Desire is the cause of all suffering." I had often wondered how someone as wise as Buddha could have thought that. How could desire ever cause suffering? Attachment and "misunderstood desire" do that. Perhaps some Puritan ethics got mixed up with Buddha's wisdom.

Wanting something, coupled with the belief that you cannot have it, or that you are foolish to want it, can cause some powerful suffering. But not desire alone. Desire, imagination, creation, anticipation—that stuff is all fun.

Desire functions as an inner sense of direction. It may be all we will ever need to know to guide us through life—to learn all that we need to know, to show up where we need to be. At least I cannot think of a more reliable guide. What else is there—someone else's desire? Somebody else's idea about what you should do? Your desire, your awareness of what you welcome offers the best compass for finding your way through the mystery of life that I have found so far. I am open to learning more or better ways. In the meantime, when I am happy and clear, I do what I am aware of wanting to do. Since I do not know what will happen around each bend, I correct my course as new information becomes available. When I am unhappy and unclear, I am grateful for Option to help me find a good starting place again.

This system of navigation pretty much eliminates regret and guilt. It also banishes the temptation to try to make anyone else suffer.

When you follow your conscious desire as an inner sense of direction, correcting your course as you go, all you have to do when you want a change is ask yourself, "What do I welcome now? Where shall I go from here?"

You can skip that part about feeling bad, worrying that you will never change, blaming someone else for your predicament. You can bypass the frantic search for a new game plan before you even know what game you want to play.

When you are un-happy about something (remember that un-happy is that general term for any feeling you do not like having) ask yourself what you welcome instead. We often become un-happy when things are *other* than the way we would like them to be. Our un-happiness can function as an alert that we have wandered off course. When used that way, our un-happiness will probably never last more than a few seconds. We will simply tune in to what we welcome and go on from there. That awareness of welcoming adds delight to the journey.

Practice Page

1. *Think of something you are un-happy about.* What do you want instead? What do you welcome into your life instead of the way it is now—instead of what you are un-happy about?

2. *Focus on what you want.* If you want that (whatever you come up with), then why are you un-happy about not having it? Or, why are you unhappy that it is not the way you want it yet? Another way to ask is: if you do not have what you want, why is un-happy the way to feel?

   Try lots of ways to ask this because it is one of the most stupid-making sets of question in Option.

3. *Write a "Blue Sky List."* If you could get it out of the clear blue sky, what would you want? If you did not have to do anything, or know how to do it, or deserve it, and if no one would ever know that you asked for it, what would you want?

You are the expert on your own life

Trusting Yourself/Self Authorization

You may not have all the answers and you may be very confused at times, but I'll bet you always do the best you can. Fresh insight or new information changes that "best you can" in a flash. A fair number of people have recoiled at that idea. About the same number embraced it each time we explored their particular issues and beliefs together.

What might it be like to live each day from that perspective?

People often approach the idea of self-trust by attempting a program of self-deception. It does not work. Telling yourself a bunch of stuff that you would like to believe but don't just slows you down and bumps you off course. Such an affirmation, one that is not true for you, which does not ring true to your ears, jars your whole being. It puts you in the position of liar and lied to simultaneously.

One of my students shared a funny but poignant example of such an affirmation in a group one night. She said, "Well if I'm getting better and better every day in every way, when the hell am I going to be any damned good at all?"

Affirming who you are and what you welcome does not require you to lie or bluff. There is always something true you can say that will help you to grow.

Begin with what you welcome anytime you get stuck, even if that is "I welcome feeling like I'm any damned good at all!"

For example: "I welcome health" might ring more true than "I create radiant, perfect health."

"I welcome financial ease" vs. "I have an infinite supply of abundance."

Both statements may be true in each case, but one may match your reality better at this point. Start with what you can say truthfully now with enthusiasm and create from there.

Whether you seek advice from the stars, numbers, psychologists, channels, books, parent, pastors, priests, mentors, gurus or the *National Enquirer*, who is going to decide which advice is wise and worth taking and which is off-base and best to avoid?

Mildred Smith, one of the co-founders of GROW presented a definition of trust that I never forgot. She said that trust is a combination of my reasonable expectation of you (based on my knowledge of you so far) and my reasonable expectation of myself (based on my knowledge of myself so far) to withstand the consequences if I am wrong about you.

That is one long complicated sentence there! But it sums up lessons it could take years to learn.

If you apply Mildred's axiom to trusting yourself, it goes something like this: Can you follow your desire as an inner sense of direction and still feel okay even if you do not like the results? Can you withstand the consequences of not knowing today what you will learn tomorrow?

This axiom provides an excellent formula to make choices with. Sometimes you may answer; sure I could be fine either way. At other times the risk-to-reward ratio may convince you to make a different choice.

You are the expert on your own life. No one knows as much about your life as you do. Other people may have a wealth of experience and knowledge for you to draw on, but in the matter of your life, whom could you trust more than yourself? If spirituality is important to you, this includes your ability to discover God's will.

For me, trusting myself means that I know I'm in my own corner, that I am dancing as fast as I can, that I want good things for myself and others. I may not have all of the answers, but I am learning as fast as I can. I am open to new insights and I welcome them.

The ultimate in self-trust is self-authorization—to flat-out authorize yourself to be you. As the Indian philosopher, Jiddu Krishnamurti asked, "Do you want freedom or a revolution within the prison?"

Who is in charge of how you feel? Exercising your emotional options requires a certain audacity. The common version of reality tells us that events and circumstances cause our feelings, as if we were just helpless puppets laughing and crying on cue. You will be swimming against the tide of popular opinion, defying reality, as most people accept it. It is not always easy.

You know the old phrase, "he pushed my buttons?" Marvin Beck and I talked about that long ago. I said something like, "Oh I know I'm responsible for having the button, but he's responsible for pushing it." Choosing from an assortment of nicknames he had for me, Marvin grinned and said, "No, Mandella, you make the button, you keep it there, and then *you* push it yourself. The other people are just doing what they do." I struggled briefly and gave in. He was just dead right.

If you want to achieve a great deal of emotional freedom very quickly, spend a few days claiming responsibility for your feelings as they arise in different situations. Say to yourself or out loud to an accepting friend, "I'm making myself angry about that." Or announce, "Now I am saddening myself about..." See if it rings true. The one that amuses me no end is to announce, "I make myself crazy about that." As opposed to the habitual, "It makes me crazy" or the all too familiar, "It drives me crazy."

Choosing to take responsibility for your own emotions puts you in charge of your life in a way few people ever experience.

This small book contains the tools to find out for yourself, what you believe, and how you want to feel. You will have to authorize yourself to use them though. And you will have to trust yourself to exercise your emotional options.

Practice Page

1. Answer this question: Am I doing the best I can with what I know and what I believe?

2. If your answer is no, see if you can find an example of a time when you could have done better with what you knew then and what you believed then.

3. Write a "Personal Declaration of Independence."

4. Write that title at the top of your page. Begin your first sentence with, "I declare my independence from...and write as long as you like.

5. Date your declaration and sign it.

Some Words of Encouragement

Here are the four easiest ways to be happy. Go for the easy way first. Take the straight shot.

The Four Easiest Ways to be Happy

1. If you want happiness, don't worry, be happy! If that doesn't work...

2. Choose happiness. If that still doesn't do it...

3. Focus on your desire. Move toward what you want. If that doesn't work...

4. Write an Option Dialogue or get someone to help you with one.

When I first began to use Option, I tried to use it on other people first. I misused it a hundred ways. I tried to get other people to become happier so that I could feel okay. And it still worked!

If these ideas appeal to you use them! It's sort of like Yoga, or breathing; it doesn't work very well if you only do it once or twice.

Fool around with these exercises and ideas. Discover your own Option Method. One of the wonderful things about Option is that it is non-invasive. It does no harm, gives no bad advice. If you do not hit the exact, perfect question, the unhappiness will simply still be there.

If you forget to be accepting, it just won't work, that's all.

Bruce Di Marsico once said, "There really isn't a *method*. It's just what you would come up with if you addressed un-happiness this way—if you are un-happy, maybe it is because you believe you have to be. Let's look together and see."

In *Emotional Options* I have covered the bases as best I can so that you can tell where to look for your own answers. You can come up with your own method as you learn, grow, and become happier.

These guidelines have worked well for me:

- Work on your own un-happiness first.

- Always return to acceptance

- Stick to the basic Option questions until you are comfortable with them. Use them like scales to practice on a piano.

- Have fun.

- When you work with yourself, writing the dialogue down helps to get you through the "getting stupid" phase.

- Follow your desire and correct your course as new information becomes available.

To your happiness!

Where It Came From

Bruce Di Marsico began to teach Option at GROW, (Group Relations Ongoing Workshops) on West Eighty Second in New York City.

I enrolled in the Group Counselors Certificate Program at Grow in November of 1970 and graduated in December of 1972.

A required course for the Group Counselors Certificate, "Overview of Methodologies" included a brief introduction to Option. After taking that course in 1971, I signed up for everything about Option I could.

Then I joined Bruce's private therapy group. When he later formed his own invitational training group I joined that too. He was developing a method to train others to teach his perspective on life.

Bruce Di Marsico first called his courses at GROW Option Therapy. Later, he called it the Option Method. Option Process was another name used. Bruce trained a group of approximately twelve people in weekly meetings at his home in Montclair, New Jersey. I say approximately because about eighteen of us started out. Some left. Others joined. We used to joke about there being twelve of us, like apostles, during one long time when we remained a constant group. Our training also required participation in a weekly therapy group to work on our own problems and issues.

Barry Neil Kaufman, who has written several books about Option, and I were in that training group. Barry's wife, Suzi, joined the group near its end, shortly after I left to move to High Falls, New York.

The Kaufman's now head the Option Institute and Fellowship in Massachusetts. They have service marked the name *Option Process.*

In 1986 I moved to California and founded Option Learning Experiences in Encinitas, on the coast just north of San Diego.

Bruce Di Marsico taught in New York City and in Montclair, New Jersey for many more years. He died in December of 1995.

I studied Option with Bruce as a fully developed, comprehensive method. My desire is to credit and acknowledge him as the founder and creator of the Option Method. I want to express my gratitude for all that I learned from him without misrepresenting him because of things I may have misunderstood or changes I have made as a result of my own considerable experience in a life which has been permanently and happily altered by the knowledge and practice of Option.

The following resource pages list some of the books and organizations available to help you to expand your knowledge of this remarkable way of living happily.

Resources

Travelling Free: How to Recover from the Past by Changing Your Beliefs by Mandy Evans (Yes You Can Press). Based on the Beyond the Past workshop, filled with workshop-tested exercises. During painful times we often form beliefs that we continue to live by without realizing it. This book tells the reader how to uncover those hidden beliefs and free themselves from them.
To order: Amazon.com or 800-431-1579.

Choosing Happiness: Mandy Evans Live at Interface (Yes You Can Press). Funny and insightful, includes actual dialogues with participants.
To order: 800-431-1579

The Principles and Philosophy of The Option Method by Bruce Di Marsico edited by Deborah Mendel and Frank Niccoletti (Dragonfly Press).
To order: Contact Deborah Mendel at www.optionmethodnetwork.com or Amazon.com

The Attractor Factor by Joe Vitale (John Wiley & Sons). Due out soon.
For information: Joe Vitale, www.mrfire.com

The Option Method Network (Hautman Web Design) contains information about the Option Method and a list of practitioners who use the Option Method.
For information: www.optionmethodnetwork.com

Lenora Boyle, Director of Option Central. Workshops, groups, and individual Option sessions. www.changelimitingbeliefs.com or 641-472-0414

Kaitryn and Steven Wertz
www.specialsolutions.net and
www.autism-programs.com

For information about workshops and training, or to book Mandy Evans for a talk or course: www.mandyevans.com or 760-416-3355

Option Learning Experiences
PO Box 337
Desert Hot Springs, CA 92264

Author Bio

Mandy Evans draws on over thirty years of experience helping people to be happier by finding and changing the beliefs that hold them back.

In addition to *EMOTIONAL OPTIONS,* she is the author of *TRAVELLING FREE: How to Recover from the Past by Changing Your Beliefs.*

She has a son, Barnaby Dorfman and now lives in Palm Springs, California.

Emotional Options

Printed in the United States
27817LVS00007BA/25

9 780976 090137